Discover other cultures

Games
Around The World

Meryl Doney

W
FRANKLIN WATTS
LONDON•SYDNEY

About this book

Games are like a universal human language. All over the world, people get together to play and enjoy games. Yet many of these games started life in quite another time and in quite a different culture.

Children, in particular, are great inventors and players of games. Many everyday things can be used to make up a game: a games board can be scratched in the sand, drawn on a rock or marked into a piece of wood; a pitch for hopscotch can be chalked onto the pavement; a bowl for a game of marbles can be dug in the ground with a heel. Simple materials can be made into dice, cards and game pieces. All you need is a few people and some simple rules, and the game is under way.

In this book we have drawn together as many different kinds of game as possible. They range from marbles and dice to the ultimate board game, chess. In between there is a rich variety of games that are taken from many countries, together with maps to show where each game comes from. This selection represents only a fraction of the games in the world. If you would like to find out more about games, look on page 30.

Most of the steps used to make the games are very easy to follow, but where you see this sign ask for help from an adult.

How to play

When you have made your games you will need to know how to play each one. You will find simple rules for the games on pages 28–29. You can play some of the games on your own, but most of them need two or more players.

This series 2005

First published as *World Crafts: Games*
Design and illustration © Franklin Watts 1997, 2005
Text © Meryl Doney 1997, 2005

Franklin Watts
96 Leonard Street, London EC2A 4XD

Franklin Watts Australia
Level 17/207 Kent Street, Sydney, NSW 2000

ISBN: 0 7496 6325 1

Dewey Decimal Classification 745.592

Series editor: Kyla Barber
Editor: Jane Walker
Design: Visual Image
Cover design: Jonathan Hair
Artwork: Ruth Levy
Photography: Peter Millard

With special thanks for help and games from Alison Croft, Ellie and Lewis Doney, Helen Miles, Willie Williams and Barnet Multicultural Study Centre.

A CIP catalogue record for this book is available from the British Library

Printed in Dubai

Contents

The world at play   4
Your own games-making kit

All kinds of dice —
India, North America & Mexico   6
Make your own dice

Marbles — Britain, France & Bangladesh   8
Make a marble bridge game

Jacks — Kenya & Europe   10
Make sets of jacks

Tops — Japan, India & Europe   12
Make a spinning top

Domino games — China & Europe   14
Make your own dominoes

Games for skilful hands —
North America, Israel & Japan   16
Make a cup-and-ball game

From lotto to bingo — Britain & Mexico   18
Make a game of La Loteria

A pack of cards —
India, Europe, Japan & North America   20
Make a set of ganjifa cards

Bean games — Burkina Faso & Kenya   22
Make a hinged mancala board

Racing games — India   24
Make a pachisi board

The ultimate war game — Burkina Faso   26
Make your own chess pieces

How to play   28

Useful information   30

Glossary   31

Index   32

The world at play

Most of the games that we play today can be traced all the way back to ancient times. They have developed from the religious practices of very ancient peoples. Hopscotch, for example, is related to ancient myths about labyrinths and mazes. These represented the journey of a person's soul from earth to heaven. Egyptian wall paintings show the pharaoh Ramses III playing a board game with the goddess Isis. Many games boards have been found built into temples and holy places, like those cut into the roofing slabs of the temple at Al-Qurnae in Egypt. These were probably made by builders when they should have been working!

Many card games and dice come from the custom of asking a holy person to foretell the future or decide when you should attempt an important task. A priest or shaman would throw marked arrows or sticks to find out the will of the gods or the fates. On the opposite page you can see how modern games equipment has developed from the use of marked arrows to foretell the future.

Games also help to prepare us for the skills that we need in life. The Inuit game of *ajaqaq* (see page 16) is intended to improve the hand and eye coordination that a successful hunter needs. Chess and other war games teach the skills of planning and foresight that are needed against an enemy.

In the age of modern communications, we can share the different games of the world as never before. This is good news. Games bring people together. At their best they allow us to use our wits and skills against each other in good-natured contest. They help to increase our understanding and enable us to form friendships. And, most of all, games are fun!

Your own games-making kit

The equipment that you need to play most of the games in this book is very simple and easy to make. If you plan to make quite a few games, you might like to collect together the most useful items of equipment and keep them in one place. Here are some recommended items for your games-making kit:

hammer · tenon saw · hacksaw · awl · hand drill · needle-nosed pliers · scissors · craft knife · metal ruler · brushes · white emulsion · poster paint · varnish · PVA (white glue) · tube of strong glue · plastic modelling material ·

modelling clay · sticky tape · masking tape · card · paper · tissue paper · newspaper · pen · pencil · felt pens · fabric and felt · needle and thread · newspaper to work on · card to cut on · apron · paper towels for cleaning up

From arrows to playing cards

Many of the game pieces that we use today began with marked arrows. These were used to foretell the future. The arrows slowly developed into smaller, more portable objects such as marked sticks or knucklebones.

 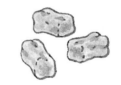 

These objects were the ancestors of a wide variety of dice and number wheels for gambling and games of chance.

Later, games of skill such as drafts, *pachisi* and chess developed. They were also played with small games pieces and dice.

In the Far East, the marked gambling sticks were replaced by strips of oiled paper. Later, these became the decorated playing cards that we use today.

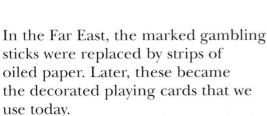  

All kinds of dice

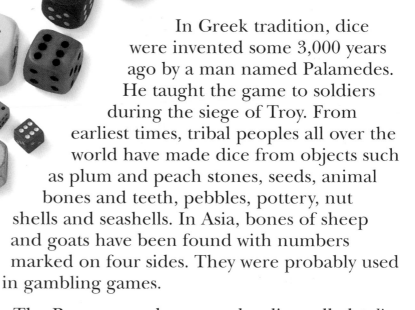

In Greek tradition, dice were invented some 3,000 years ago by a man named Palamedes. He taught the game to soldiers during the siege of Troy. From earliest times, tribal peoples all over the world have made dice from objects such as plum and peach stones, seeds, animal bones and teeth, pebbles, pottery, nut shells and seashells. In Asia, bones of sheep and goats have been found with numbers marked on four sides. They were probably used in gambling games.

The Romans used rectangular dice called *tali* as well as cube-shaped ones called *tesserae*. *Tesserae* were probably the forerunners of the cube-shaped dice that we use today. Oblong dice like the ones shown left, which were included in a set of *pachisi* (see page 24), are still popular in India.

A wide variety of materials are still used to make dice. The walnut-shell gambling dice (below left) are modelled on those used by Native American women of the Palute tribe. The split-cane dice come from *sholiwe,* a complex divination game played by the Zuni Indians of New Mexico. An eight-sided log die like this one (left) is used in gambling games in the USA.

Make your own dice

You will need: three walnuts • plastic modelling material • chisel • mallet • self-hardening clay • coloured beads • two bamboo canes, 16 cm long • vice • heavy craft knife • sandpaper • protective gloves • metal skewer • pliers

1 Place nut on its side on modelling material. Position chisel exactly on shell's edge. Tap sharply with mallet to split shell in two.

2 Remove nut and papery bits inside. Fill shell with self-hardening clay. Press coloured beads into the surface. Allow to dry.

3 To use the dice, throw them down and count how many fall with the beaded side up. This number is your score.

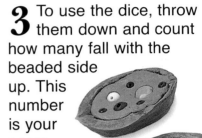

1 Grip cane in vice and split in half using heavy craft knife and mallet. Sand insides and ends smooth.

2 To add patterns, wear protective gloves and secure cane in vice. Grip skewer in pliers and hold in gas flame until very hot. Lay skewer across bamboo to make mark. End of skewer will make a dot. Repeat. Finally, run cold water over skewer to cool it.

3 To use the dice, throw them down and count the number of patterns showing.

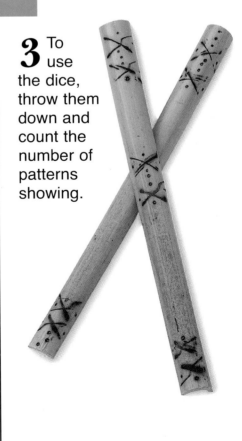

How to play ☞ **page 28**

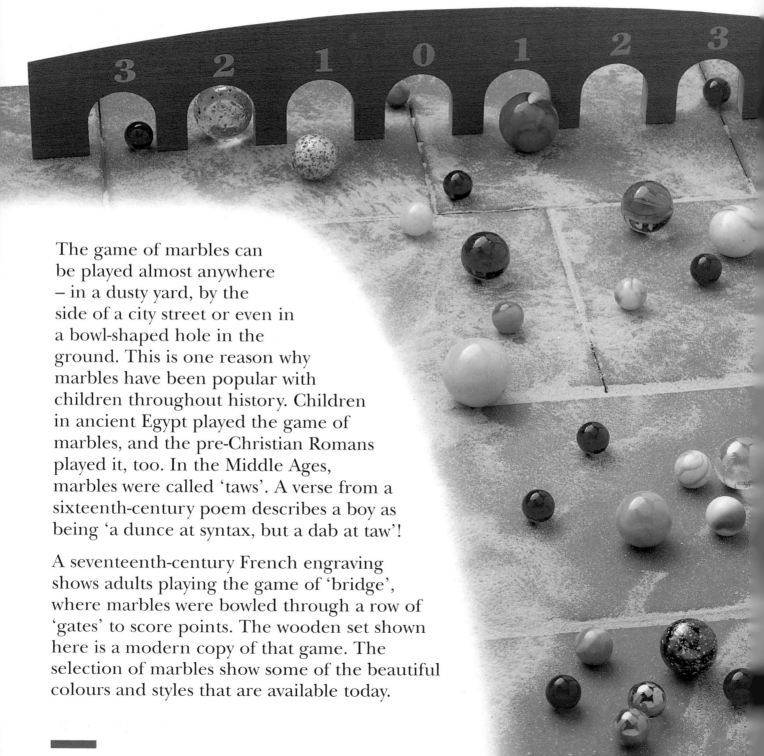

BRITAIN, FRANCE & BANGLADESH

Marbles

The game of marbles can be played almost anywhere – in a dusty yard, by the side of a city street or even in a bowl-shaped hole in the ground. This is one reason why marbles have been popular with children throughout history. Children in ancient Egypt played the game of marbles, and the pre-Christian Romans played it, too. In the Middle Ages, marbles were called 'taws'. A verse from a sixteenth-century poem describes a boy as being 'a dunce at syntax, but a dab at taw'!

A seventeenth-century French engraving shows adults playing the game of 'bridge', where marbles were bowled through a row of 'gates' to score points. The wooden set shown here is a modern copy of that game. The selection of marbles show some of the beautiful colours and styles that are available today.

Make a marble bridge game

You will need: a shoe box, 34 x 13 x 8.5 cm • ruler • pencil • compass • scissors • white emulsion paint • poster paints

Marbles are not easy to make because they have to be perfectly round. You could try making a set from self-hardening clay or bakeable modelling material. For the game to be played fairly, your opponent also needs to have home-made marbles.

2 Measure 20 mm from the edge of circle and draw another circle from that point. Continue on both sides until you have seven circles.

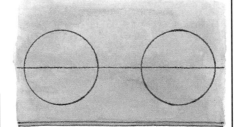

3 With scissors, cut a straight line from the bottom edge, around the circle and back down again. Repeat until you have seven arches.

4 Paint the box white. Add the score numbers above each arch and decorate with poster paints.

1 Draw a line 20 mm from the bottom edge of shoe box. Make a mark halfway along it. Set compass to 15-mm radius and draw a circle at this central point. (If your shoe box is longer, make the circles bigger. If it is shorter, draw smaller circles.)

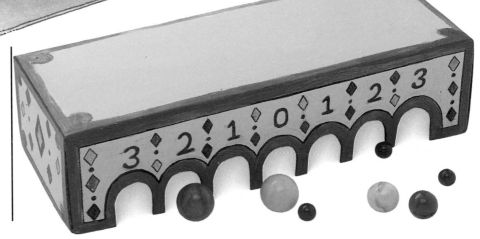

How to play ☞ page 28

Jacks

The game of jacks was originally known in Asia as 'knucklebones'. As this name suggests, the objects to be picked up were made from the knucklebones of sheep. They were called *astralogoi* by the ancient Greeks, who used them to foretell the future.

Jacks can be played with any five objects of a similar size that you can hold in the hand. The two Kenyan children below are using stones and a bowl hollowed out of the ground.

Commercially produced games of jacks are made in many different materials. These star-shaped jacks are made from metal and brightly coloured plastic. More traditional European square jacks are made from clay. New games that are based on the game of traditional jacks are always being invented for the modern toy market. For example, the pink pigs (below right) come from a game called 'Pass the Pigs'.

Make sets of jacks

Traditional European jacks were made of clay like these ones. However, you can play the game using any small and evenly weighted objects, like pebbles or beans.

You will need: two 15-mm square battens • self-hardening clay • rolling pin • flat pastry cutter • newspaper • masking tape • white glue • poster paints • varnish • five smooth pebbles • bowl • white emulsion paint

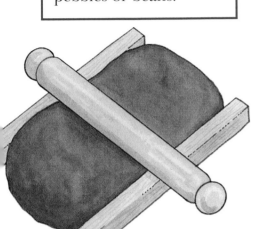

1 Place battens on either side of a lump of self-hardening clay. Roll out clay until it is flat.

2 Cut clay into five 15-mm cubes using a flat pastry cutter. Allow cubes to harden.

3 Crumple a sheet of newspaper into a ball shape. Secure with masking tape. Glue on several layers of paper pieces to form a smooth, light ball. Allow to dry. Paint and varnish.

1 Choose five pebbles of similar size and weight from the beach or garden. Wash and dry them carefully.

2 Paint pebbles all over with white emulsion. Decorate with poster paints and varnish.

How to play 👉 page 28

Tops

Any evenly balanced object can be made to spin as long as it has a point over which it will balance. Natural objects like seeds and nuts can be made to spin. Long spiral shells that are weighted at the tip are a particularly good shape for spinning. Traditionally, the Japanese are skilled top makers. Thousands of different shapes of top are possible. Modern Japanese tops, like the one shown top right, are made from turned wood or plastic, and painted in bright colours. Compare the Japanese one with the two painted tops (bottom right), which come from India.

Children still make tops from the everyday things around them. The two tops on the right, which are made from a disc of card and a pencil, and a bottle top and a nail, are similar to the ones made by Indian children. In India, wooden clubs were turned upside down and spun using a piece of thread wound around them. This idea was developed further in Japan and Europe, as seen in the plain wooden top (below). A 'handle' is used to hold the top upright, and the string is pulled to spin the top.

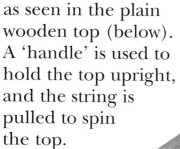

Make a spinning top

Look around at home to see what you can make into a spinning top. Experiment with lots of different shapes. Your top must be perfectly balanced to work properly, and the spindle must pass directly through the middle.

Try out your tops until you find a good balance between the size of the disc and the length of the spindle. Here are a few ideas to get you started.

1 Cut the centre piece from the CD case with wire cutters. Glue to centre of CD.

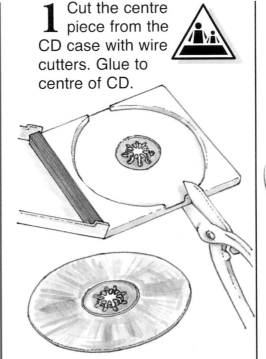

2 Find a used felt or plastic pen or a pencil that fits tightly into the centre hole. If it moves around in the hole, glue in place.

1 Choose a smooth, even cork. Make a hole directly through the centre with a knitting needle.

2 Remove the burned head of the match and sharpen end to a point with a craft knife. (Remember to cut away from yourself.)

3 Push match through the cork. If the top is too light to spin properly, add some plastic modelling material around the base of the cork.

Domino games

The game that we associate most strongly with China is mah-jong, a kind of dominoes. The name is said to come from the whispering and chirping sounds made by *mah* 'the flax plant' and *jong* 'the sparrow'. A typical mah-jong set, like the one below, contains 144 tiles made of ivory, bone, bamboo, wood or plastic. When the tiles are shuffled or 'washed', the sound produced is called 'the twittering of the sparrows'. The game is played all over China, and throughout the world wherever Chinese people settle.

The European game of dominoes is similar to mah-jong. However, it may have developed separately in Italy, spreading across Europe during the eighteenth century. Like mah-jong, domino tiles (also called 'bones' or 'stones') are directly descended from dice. The 28 tiles in a set represent all the possible throws of a pair of dice. The first tiles were originally made from bone. Later, the bone was glued to a strip of black ebony wood and fixed with a brass bolt (shown right).

Make your own dominoes

This method of making dominoes involves pressing clay into drilled holes. You could make a set of dominoes more simply by painting the dots directly onto wood with gloss paint.

You will need: 25 x 8 mm wooden batten, 140 cm long · pencil · ruler · vice · tenon saw · hand drill and countersink drill bit · self-hardening clay (coloured) · damp sponge · sandpaper or sanding block

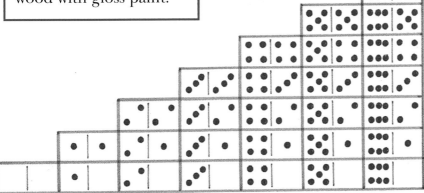

4 When completely dry, sand surface smooth. Grip batten in vice and saw across each double division to make individual dominoes. Sand edges smooth.

1 Mark batten into 25-mm divisions. Grip batten in vice and saw a shallow mark across the surface of the wood along each division line. Mark number dots as shown in the diagram above.

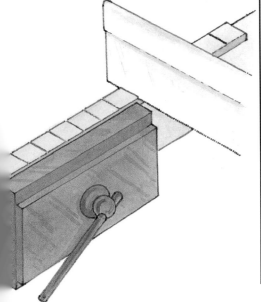

2 Using a countersink drill bit, make a shallow hole at each dot.

3 Press self-hardening clay into the holes and divisions. Wipe clay smooth with a damp sponge.

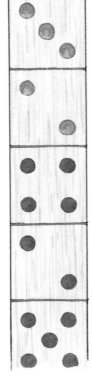

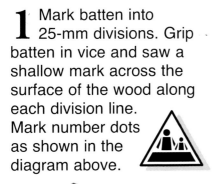

How to play 👉 page 28

Games for skilful hands

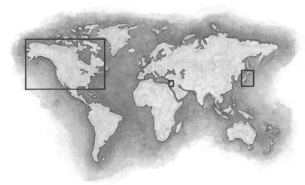

These games are used by one player at a time and they demand both skill and practice. The cup and ball was named *bilboquet* in France (from *bille* 'a wooden ball' and *boquet* 'the point of a spear'). King Henri III liked to play the game as he wandered around Paris.

A similar style of game is important for the Canadian Inuit, who call it *ajaqaq* (shown left). It is played during the dark Arctic winter. The Inuits believe that the game has magical powers to bring the return of the sun in spring.

The Japanese cup and ball (below left) has two cups and a point to trap the ball. The cup and ball (below right) is from Israel. Jewish children play with this game during the feast of Hanukkah.

Make a cup-and-ball game

You will need: large, American-style spare rib bone · saucepan of water · knife · bleach · self-hardening clay · poster paints · varnish · strong glue · cotton thread

1 From the bones left over after a meal of American-style spare ribs, choose one with a large cup-shaped end. Boil the bone in water for 10 minutes. Allow to cool.

2 With a knife, scrape away all the pieces of meat and sinew left on the bone. Leave to soak in cold water mixed with a capful of bleach for a further 10 minutes.

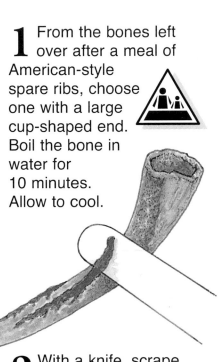

3 Using self-hardening clay, form a ball that will fit into the cup end of your bone.

Make a hole in one side of ball. Leave to dry.

Paint and varnish ball.

4 Glue cotton thread into hole in ball. Tie other end around middle of bone.

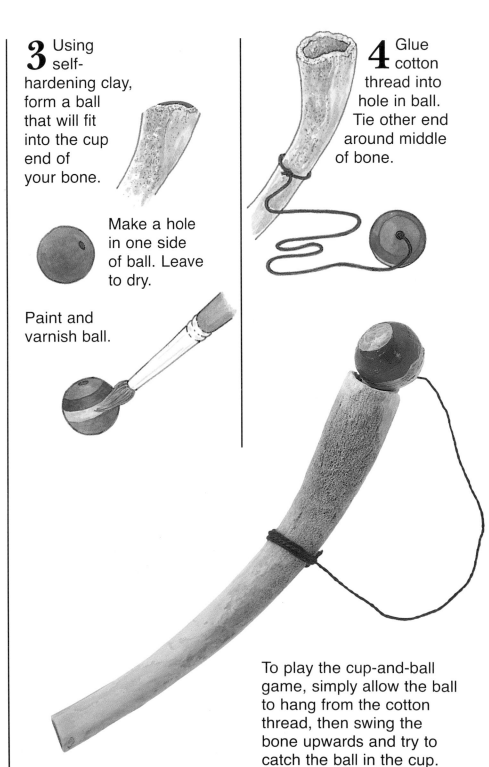

To play the cup-and-ball game, simply allow the ball to hang from the cotton thread, then swing the bone upwards and try to catch the ball in the cup.

Britain & Mexico

From lotto to bingo

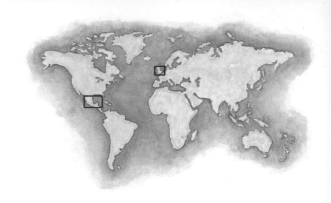

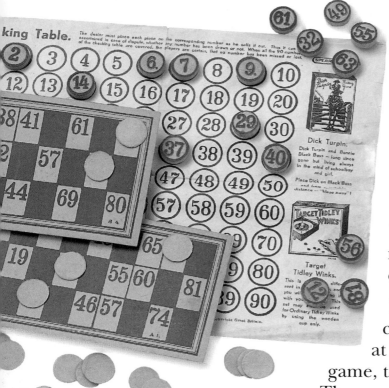

Throughout Britain, the game of bingo is played in clubs, seaside resorts and bingo halls. The old set on the left was made in Bavaria, Germany, for the Speare Game Company in Britain. This version was known as 'lotto' or 'house'. Today, bingo is played for prizes, using electronic scoreboards and special devices for tumbling the balls. The caller makes the game entertaining by giving some numbers special names, like 'legs eleven' and 'clickety click, sixty-six'.

In Mexico, a game of picture lotto called *La Loteria* is played, particularly at festivals, fairs and carnivals. In this game, too, the pictures have interesting names. The rooster, for example, is called with the phrase, 'I sing for St Peter', and the sun is the 'coat of the poor'. When the picture card of the Devil comes up, the caller says, 'Sweet Virgin Mary'! Verses are sometimes shouted out when the Devil is called.

Make a game of *La Loteria*

This is a simple method of making a lotto set if you don't want to draw your own pictures. If you are studying another language, write the picture names in that language. Playing the game will help you to learn the names of everyday objects.

You will need: two sheets of A4 paper • pencil • ruler • craft knife • magazines • scissors • paper paste • use of a colour photocopier • thin card • cotton reel • poster paints

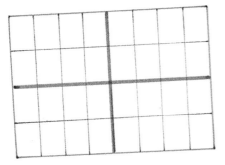

1 Divide sheet of A4 paper in half lengthways and widthways, and draw heavy lines across. Divide each rectangle again into eight sections as shown.

2 On another piece of paper, mark a rectangle 37 x 52.5 mm. Cut out with a craft knife to form a window.

3 Use window to select simple pictures from magazines. Draw around the inside of the window with a pencil. Cut out 32 pictures in this way.

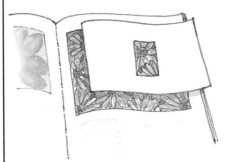

4 Paste each picture into a rectangle to form a patchwork of images. On a colour photocopier, enlarge the A4 sheet to A3 size and make a colour copy of it.

5 Cut out the individual pictures from the original A4 sheet. Cut A3 sheet along the heavy lines into four separate sheets. Paste each sheet onto thin card.

6 Use a cotton reel and pencil to draw 32 circles on a sheet of thin card. Cut out the circles. Divide them into four sets of eight discs, and paint each set a different colour.

How to play 👉 page 29

A pack of cards

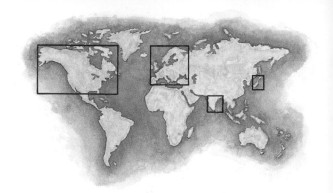

Playing cards probably developed from the marked arrows that were used long ago to foretell the future (see page 5). Originally, the shafts were painted with emblems. In time these emblems were copied onto gambling sticks, then onto strips of oiled paper and finally onto linen boards.

India's traditional cards, like this set from Orissa (left), are called *ganjifa*. They are hand painted on lacquered cloth. The Hindu god *Ardhanari* is shown on early Indian cards with a cup, a sceptre, a sword and a ring. These symbols are very similar to the four suits of the European tarot cards (cups, batons, swords and coins). The cards may have been brought to Europe from Asia by gypsies, who were originally nomads in India.

European playing cards were first printed in the fifteenth century. This Spanish poker set (near left) has coins, cups, swords and clubs. France introduced the traditional *coeur* (heart), *trèfle* (club), *pique* (spade) and *carreau* (diamond). More recently, packs have been designed using many different themes. They can even teach a subject, like this Black History deck (near left).

Make a set of *ganjifa* cards

This set of cards has been designed around the Creation story from the Book of Genesis in the Bible. There is one symbol for each of the seven days. Use your set to play a game of snap. You may like to make a special box, like the one shown opposite, to keep your cards in.

You will need: good-quality A4 cartridge paper • pencil • ruler • compass • poster paints • felt pens • varnish or sheet of sticky plastic • scissors

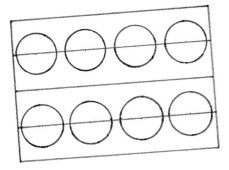

1 Divide A4 paper lengthways into four. Set compass to 35 mm and draw four circles along the top line and four along the bottom as shown. This makes a set of eight cards. Repeat until you have seven sets.

2 Paint a coloured circle in the centre of each card. Choose a different colour for each set. Add a contrasting edge colour, leaving a strip of white between the two.

3 With felt pens and paints, add a different symbol to each set of cards. You could use the seven symbols shown below, or design your own. Write a number 1 on one card in the first set, a number 2 on one in the second set, and so on.

4 Varnish cards or cover with sticky plastic. Cut out cards.

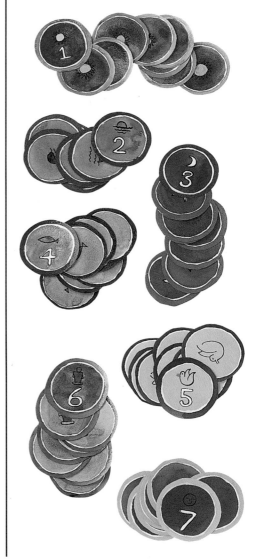

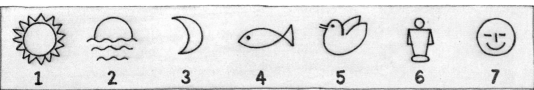

How to play ☞ page 29

Bean games

Mancala games have become associated with Africa. However, the name comes from the Arabic word *manquala*, which means 'to move', and the earliest known *mancala* boards were found in Egypt. Today the game is played across Africa, the Near East, India and as far away as Malaysia, Indonesia and the Philippines. Sometimes *mancala* is played to amuse the spirit of a dead person before burial.

Mancala is a very easy game to set up. It can be played in holes that are either dug in the ground or cut into rocks by the roadside. Dried beans, coins, pebbles or shells can be used as pieces. In Egypt it is even played with pellets of camel's dung!

This hinged board (below) comes from Burkina Faso. A children's version of the game may have three holes on each side, but the game being played by these Maasai people in Kenya (left) has many more holes. Other names for *mancala* include *congklak*, which is played in Indonesia, *gabata* in Ethiopia and *kiarabu* in Zanzibar.

Make a hinged *mancala* board

You will need: two 12-hole egg boxes • bread knife • masking tape • kitchen paper towel • PVA glue • newspaper • squares of tissue paper • brown emulsion paint • black felt pen • dried chick peas or beans

1 With a bread knife, cut off the high points from egg box. Using short strips of masking tape, cover all the holes.

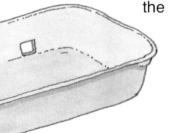

2 Cut lid from second box. Tape lid to base of first egg box.

3 Roll sheets of paper towel into balls and push one into each cup. Stick two pieces of masking tape into a cross shape. Push tape into cups to form a smooth, round base. Stick a third piece around the rim.

4 Paint egg box with PVA glue and cover it with alternate layers of newspaper, glue and tissue paper squares. Re-cut slots in the box lid for the fastening bumps. Allow to dry.

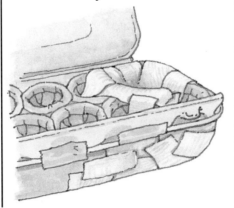

5 Paint all over with brown emulsion. Use a large felt pen to decorate box with African-style designs.

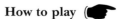

How to play ☞ page 29

Racing games

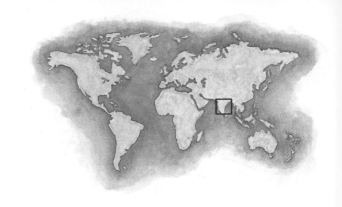

Pachisi is one of the most popular Indian games. It is really a race around a cross-shaped board. The board is usually made from cloth squares, which are often embroidered with silks and decorated with mirror work. In the palaces of northern India there are traces of large, red and white marble boards on which the Moghul emperors played *pachisi*. Their 'playing pieces' were sixteen slave girls who were dressed in different coloured saris.

In a game of *pachisi*, two, three or four players sit around the cross-shaped board, one at each arm. If four people are playing, players sitting opposite each other can be partners. Each player has four playing pieces and moves them by throwing dice.

Pieces start on the central square, which is called the *charkoni*, or throne. They must travel down their own arm of the cross, then anti-clockwise around the board. Pieces must return to the middle by the same path, avoiding capture by their opponents.

Make a *pachisi* board

Gingham or checked material is used to make this board because the squares make it easier to cut the material into shape. However, you can use any flat material in any pattern you like.

You will need: two pieces of different coloured material • scissors • length of 4-cm tape or ribbon • sewing pins • needle • sewing thread • sewing machine • length of 7-mm white tape • self-hardening clay • paints • varnish

1 Cut out two strips of material, 68 x 12 cm, and a square piece, 12 x 12 cm, in a contrasting colour.

2 Lay strips across each other. Pin and tack tape down centre of each arm of the cross. Lay the square over the centre and tack in place.

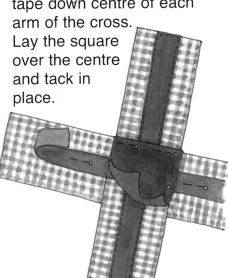

3 Use a sewing machine to attach thin white tape to the edges of the fabric. Sew more white tape across the arms of the cross to mark out squares. Mark out 'castles' with tape crosses.

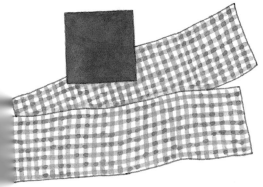

4 To make the game pieces, take 16 pieces of self-hardening clay about the size of a walnut and make into balls. Mould each ball into a bell shape. Allow to dry. Divide into four sets of four pieces and paint each set in a different colour. Varnish when dry.

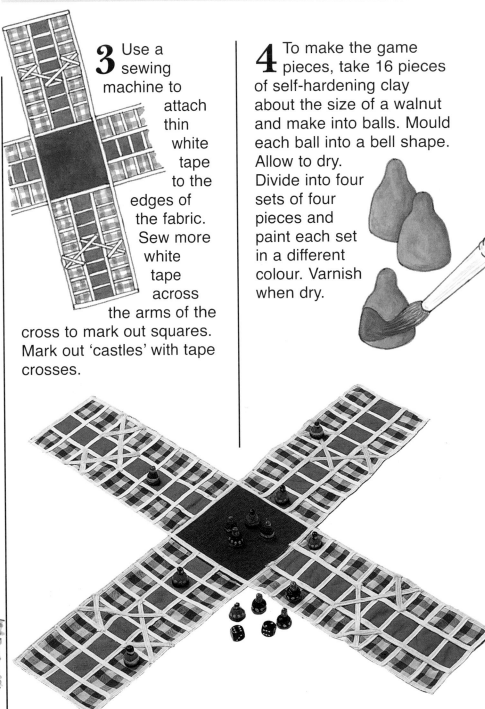

How to play ☞ **page 29**

The ultimate war game

Across the world, it is universally agreed that chess is the queen of all games. One book on the game is published somewhere in the world every day, and chess has become the national game in more than one country.

Chess was probably invented in India. It was originally a war game called *chaturanga*, which means 'four limbs' in Sanskrit. The 'limbs' were the four parts of an army: elephants, horses, chariots and foot soldiers. As the game was taken by travellers along the trade routes of the world, the pieces changed. The *shah*, a Persian name for 'ruler', became the king, the elephants became castles and the chariots changed to bishops. The king was originally supported by a vizier, or advisor. By the Middle Ages he had become the powerful queen piece.

Chess boards can be made from fine materials such as marble and silver. The figures in this set from Burkina Faso are made from cast metal.

Make your own chess pieces

1 To make a pawn, fold a pipe cleaner in half. Twist together a short way from the loop to form head. Bend two sides outwards and in again to form arms. Twist pipe cleaner together again to form body, leaving free ends as legs. Bend one end up for a foot, and leave the other straight. Twist each arm.

You will need: 50 plain, white pipe cleaners • two wine bottle corks • self-hardening clay • knife • small bowl • plaster of Paris • paints • varnish

2 To make larger pieces, use two pipe cleaners. Twist one to form head and arms. Bend other one in half around neck, twist body and fold rest in half for legs.

3 For king, add short length of pipe cleaner as a crown. Make crook or staff from pipe cleaner. For queen, twist pipe cleaner around body to make skirt. Advisors can have a turban or headdress.

4 To make horses, bend a pipe cleaner in half and form head, ears and neck. Add body and tail from another pipe cleaner. Fold two more in half for legs. Make rider as shown in step 1.

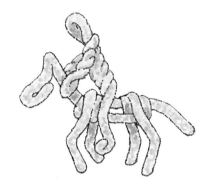

5 Form a pipe cleaner into four small square shapes with two long ends. Make a hole in one side of the top of a cork. Push both ends into hole, forming squares into castle battlements.

6 Roll out clay and cut into 16 discs. Push the straight 'long' foot of each chess piece into a disc. Leave to harden.

7 Mix up small bowl of plaster of Paris until it is like thick cream. Plunge each chess piece in turn into plaster, shake off drips and stand upright to dry. (Do this very quickly because the plaster thickens very fast.) When dry, paint and varnish.

How to play ☛ page 29

How to play...

page 7 **DROP DEAD**

■ Any number of people can play. You will need five cube-shaped dice and a cup.

■ Throw one die to decide who begins. Player 1 throws all five dice. If the player throws a 2 or a 5 there is no score, but the dice showing 2s or 5s are set aside. They are 'dead'.

■ Player 1 continues to throw the remaining dice. If there are no 2s or 5s, player 1 adds up the spots on the dice to score. The turn ends when all five dice are 'dead'. The player with the highest total is the winner.

page 9 **MARBLE BRIDGE**   **BOMBARDIER**   **IN THE POT**

■ Each player in turn rolls five marbles towards the arches. If one goes through an arch, the player scores that number. The player with the highest score is the winner.

■ Each player adds a number of marbles into a circle.

■ The first player holds a 'bomb' marble above the circle and drops it. He or she wins any marble knocked out of the circle and takes back the 'bomb'. The game ends when the circle is empty.

■ You will need a bowl-shaped hole, often dug in the ground with the heel, and a line drawn two metres from the hole.

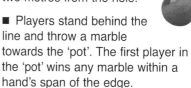

■ Players stand behind the line and throw a marble towards the 'pot'. The first player in the 'pot' wins any marble within a hand's span of the edge.

■ Any player who gets into the 'pot' has three chances to shoot the other players out and win their marbles.

page 11 **JACKS**

■ To decide who begins, each player throws five jacks into the air and tries to catch as many as possible on the back of the hand. He or she then throws the jacks up again and catches them in the palm. The player who catches the most jacks begins the game.

■ Player 1 throws the jacks on the ground. He or she throws the ball in the air and picks up one jack before catching the ball again. The player transfers this jack to the other hand and throws the ball again, picking up the jacks one by one.

■ After single jacks, the player can go on to picking up the jacks in twos, threes, fours and finally all five together. When he or she drops or moves a jack, or fails to catch the ball, then it is the turn of the next player.

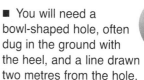

page 15 **BLIND HUGHIE**

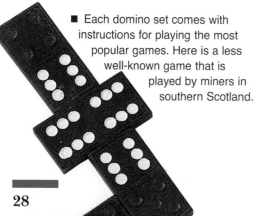

■ Each domino set comes with instructions for playing the most popular games. Here is a less well-known game that is played by miners in southern Scotland.

■ Two to five players set out five tiles each, face down, in a row. They draw tiles to decide who begins. Player 1 turns over his or her left-hand tile and puts it in the middle. Player 2 turns over his or her left-hand tile. If it matches either end of the first tile, player 2 places it beside the matching number. If not, the tile is placed face up at the right-hand end of player 2's line.

■ Play finishes when one player has used all his or her tiles. The other players then count up the number of dots on their remaining tiles. If the game stops before anyone is out, the player with the lowest number of dots is the winner.

page 19 ## LA LOTERIA

■ This is a game for two to four people and one caller. Each player has one or two game cards and some discs.

■ The caller puts the individual cards in a bag. He or she takes one card out of the bag and calls out the name of the picture, like 'cat' or 'rose'.

■ Any player with that picture on his or her game card covers it up with a disc.

■ The player who covers a row of four pictures shouts out 'lotto' or 'bingo' and wins the game.

page 21 ## SNAP

■ Deal out all the cards. Each player, in turn, lays a card face up.

■ Each time two players lay the same symbol, the first player who calls 'snap' is the winner and takes the cards.

■ If two number cards come up, the players shout 'battle'. They then throw dice or toss a coin to see who wins the cards on the table.

page 23 ## MANCALA

■ This is a simple *mancala* game for four players. First, put four beans in each hole.

■ Player 1 takes the four beans from any hole on his or her side and drops one into the next four holes in an anti-clockwise direction. When all four beans have been dropped, player 1 picks up all five beans from the last hole and begins to drop them into the next holes in the same direction. When player 1's last bean falls into an empty hole, the turn is over.

■ Player 2 takes the beans from any hole on his or her side and begins to play. As soon as a hole has four beans, the player on that side can capture them.

■ Any player dropping a last bean in a hole on his or her side, making four, can capture them but that player's turn is then over. If the same thing happens on the opponent's side, the other player captures them.

■ The game ends when eight beans or less are left on the board and each player captures those on his or her own side. The player with the most captured beans is the winner.

page 25 ## PACHISI

■ Each player throws two dice and the highest scorer begins.

■ Player 1 throws the dice and moves one piece from the *charkoni*. Players move around the board until they reach the home arm again. They must throw an exact number to re-enter the *charkoni* and win.

■ Players can be captured and returned to the *charkoni* by another player who lands on the same square. To avoid capture, players can rest on a 'castle' square or have two of their own pieces (or one of each partner's pieces) on the same square. When pieces double up in this way, they can move around the board together.

■ An opposing player can still capture these doubled-up pieces by landing two or more pieces on the same square.

■ Players can miss a turn, or go round a second time, to help their partners. The winner is the first person or team to return all their pieces to the *charkoni*.

page 27 ## CHESS

When you have made your chess pieces, you will be able to find detailed instructions on how to play chess from one of the many books on the subject in your local or school library. Borrow a board with eight by eight plain squares from another chess set, or make your own board out of card or modelling clay.

Useful information

United Kingdom

Websites

www.tradgames.org.uk
(guide to the history of different games)
www.compendia.co.uk/mancala.htm
(rules on how to play mancala)
www.hobbycraft.co.uk
(Hobbycraft also has stores all over the UK)
www.thebritishmuseum.ac.uk/compass/index.html
(see pictures of mancala boards on display at the museum)

Museums

The Cumberland Toy and
Model Museum
Banks Court
Market Place
Cockermouth
Cumbria CA13 9NG
Tel. 01900 827606
www.toymuseum.co.uk

Museum of Childhood
Cambridge Heath Road
London E2 9PA
Tel. 020 8980 2415
www.vam.ac.uk/vastatic/nmc/

Museum of Childhood, Edinburgh
42 High Street
Royal Mile
Edinburgh EH1 1TB
0131 529 4142

Australia

Online craft suppliers

www.theartshop.com.au
www.dragonflydreams.com.au
www.auscraftnet.com.au
(directory of craft suppliers)

Craft shops

Goldfields Crafts, Forbes Rd,
Leigh Creek 3352
Phone: (03) 5334 7793

Yee's Hobbies & Crafts
19 Bishop Street
Stuart Park 0820
Phone: (08) 8981 3255

Every effort has been made by the Publisher to ensure that these websites are suitable for children, and contain no inappropriate or offensive material. However, because of the nature of the Internet, it is impossible to guarantee that the contents of these sites will not be altered. We strongly advise that Internet access is supervised by a responsible adult.

Glossary

carnival A celebration or festival, especially one held just before the Christian season of Lent.

divination A way of telling what will happen in the future.

ebony A heavy black hardwood from a tropical tree.

emblem A badge or sign that belongs to a group or family.

the fates Three Greek or Roman goddesses who ruled people's lives.

forerunner A person who comes before another person to prepare for his or her arrival.

Hanukkah The Jewish festival of lights. It is celebrated for eight days during December.

ivory The white material that makes up elephant tusks.

knuckle A bone that makes up the joint at the base of each finger.

labyrinth A complicated, and often confusing, arrangement of paths and passages.

pawn A small playing piece in the front row on a chess board.

prophecy A prediction about what will happen in the future.

ritual A religious or very serious set of actions.

rooster A male chicken.

Sanskrit An Indian language that was first spoken about 3,500 years ago. It is the language of the Hindu religion.

sceptre The rod that is held by a king or queen at special ceremonies.

shaman A priest, a holy man or a witch doctor.

spindle A rod that passes through the centre of an object.

strategy A plan of action.

suit A set of playing cards with the same symbol on each card.

syntax The correct arrangement of words to make phrases and sentences.

tarot A game in which cards are used to tell a person's fortune.

turned Describes wood that has been carved on a lathe.

Index

ajaqaq 16
ancient origins 4
arrows, marked 4, 5, 20
astralogoi 10

Bangladesh 8
bean games 22
bilboquet 16
bingo 18
blind hughie game 28
bombardier game 28
books about games 30
Britain 8, 18
Burkina Faso 22, 26

card games 4, 29
chess 26–27
 rules of the game 29
chess pieces 26, 27
China 14
congklak 22
cup-and-ball game 4, 16, 17

dice 4, 5, 6–7
 dice game 28
divination games 6
dominoes 14–15
 domino game 28
drop dead game 28

Egypt 4, 8, 22
Europe 8, 10, 12, 14, 18, 20

fortune telling 4, 5, 10
France 8, 16

gabala 22
gambling sticks 5, 20
game boards 4, 23, 24, 25
games-making kit 5
ganjifa playing cards 20, 21
Greece 6, 10

hopscotch 4

in the pot game 9
India 6, 12, 20, 24, 26
Inuit 4, 16
Israel 16

jacks 10–11
 rules of the game 28
Japan 12, 16, 20

Kenya 10, 22
kiarabu 22
knucklebones 5, 10

La Loteria 18, 19
 rules of the game 29
log dice 6
lotto 18–19

mah-jong 14
mancala 22, 23
 rules of the game 29
marble bridge game 8, 9
marbles 8–9
 marble games 28
Mexico 6, 18
museum collections 30

North America 6, 16, 20
number wheels 5

pachisi 6, 24, 25
 rules of the game 29
picture lotto 18, 19
playing cards 5, 20–21

racing games 24–25
religious practices 4
Romans 6, 8

sholiwe 6
snap card game 29
spinning tops 12, 13
split-cane dice 6, 7

tarot cards 20
tops 12–13

walnut-shell dice 6, 7
war games 4, 26

Additional photographs:

page 10 (bottom), page 22 (top): Geoff Sayer, OXFAM; page 16 (top): © British Museum.